ONCE A Girl, NOW A Woman

NIKKI ROWE

BALBOA.
PRESS
A DIVISION OF HAY HOUSE

Balboa Press books may be ordered through booksellers or by contacting:

Balboa Press
A Division of Hay House
1663 Liberty Drive
Bloomington, IN 47403
www.balboapress.com.au
1-(877) 407-4847

ISBN: 978-1-4525-1040-8 (sc)
ISBN: 978-1-4525-1041-5 (e)

Printed in the United States of America

Balboa Press rev. date: 06/12/2013

To my love, my life my soul, my heart—Xavier,

my boisterous three-year-old.

CONTENTS

PREFACE

$\mathcal{B}$e yourself, understand yourself, accept yourself, and love yourself.

If you have picked up this book, it is no coincidence; you have come to find/create yourself.

This book is for *all* the beautiful souls in this world who have come to find themselves, create themselves, and live for themselves.

This is my journey, in which I am speaking my deepest thoughts and trusting that my readers will understand me.

If I can heal *one* soul through my words, then my job is done.

Peace. Love. Gratitude.

XO

ACKNOWLEDGEMENTS

Without my son, Xavier, this book would never have been completed. Most ask, "How did you do it?" I respond with, "How could I not learn a new way of life with such a courageous little soul to live for?"

Thank you to my beautiful mother; many of us say we have the best mothers in the world, and I am definitely among them. Throughout my darkest nights and gloomiest days, she has helped me, encouraged me, and inspired me to continue on my journey. This woman has seen the darkest of days and still knows how to smile contagiously. Having such an inspiring woman support and love me unconditionally has given me the strength I needed.

To my dad (Scoot), you are truly a blessing in our little family's lives. Thank you for your unconditional support and love of life, with an added *big* thank-you to my father in heaven for sending such a beautiful soul to complete what you couldn't.

Last but not least, my brother—thank you for helping me realise my true potential. You broke me and helped raise me, and for this, I will always love you. You are a blessing in my life. We have a brother–sister bond that will continue to grow throughout our entire lives. I'm so proud of you.

Jessica Thehu—if you have met this lady, hold on to her tight. She is a one of the most enchanting ladies I know. She is my best friend, my soul sister.

My cherished friends and family are true beauties, and I am blessed to have them as a part of my life. My ladies got me through my days and nights—filling my heart with laughter and love and helping me believe in myself when the darkest nights were filling my world.

I also thank the people I loved and lost; they will always hold a place in my book of life. I am thankful for the pain, the sadness, the vulnerability, the happiness, the contentment, the understanding, and the knowledge I have gained; this life truly is beautiful if you can look beyond your own imagination.

INTRODUCTION

*S*o here it goes . . .

Sometimes we sit and wonder whether we're on the path we'd always imagined—whether the road we are looking down will truly fill our heart's desire or whether, by chance, just by chance, we are following the instinct that is stronger than upbringing.

Only we will know where our own hearts stand. The longer you ignore your own intuition, the longer you'll live to suffer pain in this universe. It may take months or even years to complete our karmic journeys, but as we will all learn, it's the higher understanding of conscious living that keeps us growing towards our truer selves.

So many sit and ponder, wondering why and how their life could be different or why it is the way it is.

The answer is simple and, most of the time, right in front of us.

You.

You are the answer.

So when you slowly lose your faith in your own being, remember one thing—nothing in this world is wrong; you are always where you're supposed to be.

Whether you are living through heartache or complete happiness, you are supposed to be there at that exact moment. Each emotion we are feeling, each situation that we attract in our lives reflects on the soul inside.

Growth is the most important journey of you.

So you now ask where to start. How do you start looking within to find the answers? How do you speak to yourself?

The answer is easy, yet it will be the hardest journey of your life.

Welcome to the life of living real truths, real answers.

In this book, you may see that the truth is ugly and bare. Remember, though, that heartbreak from truth is a better experience than happiness from lies.

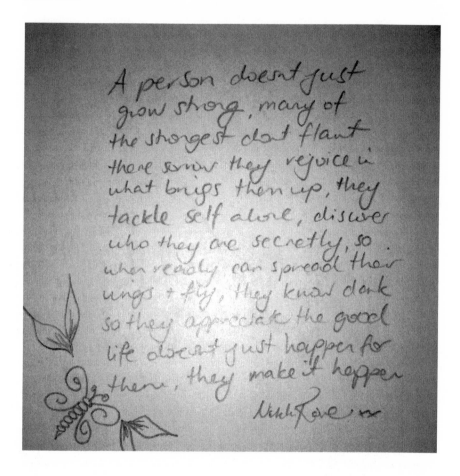

*   *   *

I dance to the beat of the earth;
The memories are the lyrics I write;
Nature leads my soul
Through this existence I call life.

CHAPTER 1

RECOGNISE

F or so long, many of us have been on a journey to discover our deepest truths. We all get tired of living in a world so routine, where material possessions seem to win out over the power of love. We often get so caught up in it all that we find ourselves eventually realising we are not fulfilling our true lives and that we are living for others.

We so often live in fear of judgement; it is a fear that we will let down all those who have ever loved us. We slowly allow these thoughts and fears, as well as our egos, to change our own perceptions of what we wish our lives would be. We continue time after time to forget our own worth. Many of us are raised to grow up and go to college, get a job, marry someone we love, have children, continue a generation, and then pass on. We don't take risks, and we don't redeem opportunities.

What kind of a life is this?

Will we one day look back at our lives and believe that we did everything we were supposed to do, or will we realise we have really been living for another?

So ask yourself, from deep within your heart, what is your truth?

What are your feelings? Are you feeling hurt, angry, anxious, depressed, nervous, impatient, insecure, misunderstood, unworthy, or ashamed?

You are not alone.

Recognising these feelings allows you to grow. It will give you strength that will help you to understand and gain a deeper knowledge of yourself.

How can you ever discover who you are if you don't recognise the real, honest truth of your feelings first?

You may be familiar with some of the feelings that arise; others, you won't recognize. Many of us don't truly know what it is to be completely happy, to feel accepted, or to be in a genuinely loving atmosphere. Some of us are ten steps ahead at a very young age. Regardless of the journey we wish to undertake, our background and are choices will all direct the path we wish to take in life.

Some of us go through life doing everything in our power to ignore the truth and ignore the pain—to cover it up like it never existed.

To recognise why you are feeling differently than you wish to be feeling is to be on the path of self-discovery. When you are being honest and open with yourself, it will hurt; it will start to cause emotions deep inside your soul that you never imagined. This is good; living in truth never came easy.

This feeling could be a deeply rooted loss of trust, faith, or acceptance from a childhood memory or a kind of dispute or maybe even the breakdown of a relationship or friendship. Whatever its cause, recognising that you still hold any kind of resentment can unfold your heart and open it to inner peace and true acceptance.

Our hearts cannot feel peace if we are holding on to bad feelings stemming from memories that we need to eliminate from our minds; yes, memories are amazing. I believe they are the imprints of who we are and what we become. We must not let them overcome us, overcome our minds, and change our future realities.

* * *

Only *you* can bring yourself happiness. *You* are the creator of how you wish your life to be; others are only a part of the story.

You will never be who you are if you never let go of who you thought you were.

I walked alone, not because I had to but because I chose to. The ones who change the world do not follow; they make a path where the grass seems too long. The road is never too short, and their journeys, before they take them, are completely unheard of. Be different. Be daring. Be real.

*   *   *

*   *   *

There is a difference between a glimpse of a memory and living through the memory.

You will learn to recognise this difference in the journey—to recognise whether the feeling is from a memory you are reliving or from a memory you have not yet accepted and let go of.

If the situation you are remembering still brings feelings other than contentment and peace to your heart, then you are still in the process of healing this negative energy.

By living through the memory, you are growing hate, anger, and deep emotions of resentment and anguish. You are slowly closing your heart to its true potential as you hold on to these lost feelings. You are choosing your path of fate without realising it.

Someday, these emotions will come back in forms other than those they started in. At this present moment, I ask you to freely write your thoughts on paper including all your fears and negative feelings regarding any situations you are still holding on to.

Remembering a memory is powerful; in any situation, no matter what it is, you should always embrace open communication and open memories.

Talking about our memories helps us understand and recognise who we are, what we have learnt, and what we accept for our future lives. Memories are in the past; they are the purest reactions of you.

Memories are beautiful; cherish them.

If you meet a soul who gives you problems as you relive memories about him or her, that person doesn't deserve you.

We are born pure, content, and loving. We are all the same—filled with acceptance, harmony, and grace.

Each one of us has different lessons and guidance embedded into our minds and thought processes. So as we age, we all deal with different experiences in such different ways. This is no reason to give up on our futures or to use a tough past as an excuse. Everything that happens to each and every one of us is a lesson—either a karmic rebirth or a lesson that will change our minds and help us reach a higher consciousness.

We are all on this earth together—not in competition with one another, but to congregate together as one with the loving energy, we all need to heal in this life.

We are all on a journey to complete our souls, to recognise that we are here on earth to feel pure and loving.

There are many ways to start to recognise your emotions and feelings. (Must I state that it is okay to know how you are feeling? Who are you to ignore your own emotions? Always remember that we attract what we are.)

Art is one of the many ways to tap into self-discovery; it allows your conscious mind and your subconscious to work as one.

Write a dream on paper and imagine optimism in the now and for the future.

What has come of your past and all the lessons you've encountered? Moreover, how much have you grown from these experiences? Once you start recognising your emotions from a higher perspective, stepping outside your own mind, you can get a clear indication of what needs attention and what you should dismiss. The key you hold will now open you up to many deep discoveries.

*   *   *

All of us would succeed in life
if we lived through our hearts filled with love.
Escape the hate that fills your state of being, your mind, and your soul.
Live in freedom and peace, and create who you wish to be.

*   *   *

TASK 1: DREAM BOARD

In this first chapter, I want you to start a dream board. If you have never heard of a dream board before, it is a paper design onto which you place images of your heart's desires, your dreams, and the things that fulfil you. It is like a bucket list without including possessions you must acquire. It is a tool you can use in order to enrich your soul and imagine what you want to find within yourself.

A dream board can be any size, shape, or colour, as long as it is something you love.

In each chapter, I will be asking you to complete a task to put on this dream board. At the end of the book, you will have not only the knowledge the book offers but a beautiful board as a reminder that you are heading toward your destiny.

I also wish you to write a board on your feelings—all the feelings inside you. Please be honest with yourself; you can never truly heal if you deny the fact that you are not perfect.

No one is. Perfection lies in the ability to see through our weaknesses and faults and to love ourselves entirely.

Finish this board with one saying. You might consider starting a journal. So that each chapter helps illuminate the past, you can write down the truest emotions you felt at the time so you can look back on them.

*   *   *

RECOGNISE

When you recognise an emotion deep within your soul,
Nothing can take the pain away, and you start to feel lost.
Remember, you are already winning by seeing the emotion as it is.
No more denying your truths; you cannot run from this.
Seeing all your feelings and recognising them as they are,
You are already on the journey of self-discovery, so congratulate
yourself on your efforts so far.

CHAPTER 2

UNDERSTAND

When you have come to recognise your emotions and where you stand within yourself, you can slowly unravel the many layers of who you truly are.

Understanding does not stop at knowing why you got called into work today when you have just worked ten days straight, or why you were just involved in an accident that was caused by another party yet you have to foot the bill.

Understanding is a deep connection to our minds, bodies, and souls, in which we lie centred and pure throughout all our circumstances.

When you have an understanding of why you are feeling the way you do—why you are angry, hurt, or sad and life is not working out the way you want—right there is where you will stop!

By trying to understand why you feel the way you feel, you are already two steps ahead of yourself. Ask many questions until you come to an understanding of why. Maybe the answer is to take yourself away from the situation and realise that everything happens in its own divine timing.

Sometimes this process can take weeks or even years to fulfil; but always understand that you are already on the journey by picking up this book.

* * *

You know, when I was sitting here writing this, I slowly had a disbelief in myself that I would never be a writer, even though writing was the only thing that flowed so naturally from the tips of my fingers. Many nights I would sit and write and write, until one night came; I opened my computer screen. I had no idea what I was about to write and let my fingers do the work. Now here you are reading my dream.

* * *

Self-discovery is a challenge; it's a challenge that involves self-understanding and self-love and feeling a sense of contented peace within yourself.

When you reach the point of peace and unity with your mind, body, and soul, you will understand that you have a choice in every aspect of your life. Yes, negative influences will always try to nibble their way into your light. But in the end, what matters is how you react when the situations unfold. We all have the option to choose to understand life a little more to its core, a little more towards ourselves, and a little more within the earth.

Understanding is more about realising who you are than realising what you want.

Understanding is one step closer to acceptance. When we have a deeper understanding, we choose to react less and less to the negative impacts in our lives. We create our own beings. We can enlighten our own knowledge as to what we wish our lives to be.

Do you find yourself often wondering why we do things that bring forth many different emotions from our souls? Why do we have to hurt when we could love? Why do some smile when there's nothing to smile about? Each soul on this earth is different, yet we have one capability that is identical—*love*, and through love, we can be contented with life's raw triggers and tests.

As we understand, we learn never to regret our actions but rather to accept all wrongdoings as a lesson. So often, our actions are misguided, and this world can be too black and white.

There is no wrong versus right in this world, only ego against soul, war against love, and truth against deceit. Every choice we make leads us to our destiny; whether you're on the long road or the short road, you are always where you're meant to be at that exact moment.

Where would we find any rhythm of true peace that resembles the egotistical, impatient side of most of life's occurrences? So often, we sit and misjudge before we give ourselves the opportunity to understand. We are forever going back and forth within our egos and souls, whilst going through cleansing in our life. But has this happened many times? Trust me, I understand. I know exactly the pain you are going through. Life was never meant to be easy; it was always only meant to be worth it.

Understanding is slow, and it is patient; it is also truthful and loving. When you understand yourself and why you cause actions and reactions to outside occurrences, you can understand how to better your existence with love, to free your mind, and to allow the true essence of your soul to excel.

There is always a deeper knowing—an understanding of destiny right before our eyes. I give my blessing for you to use this tool wisely in life; let it be your true best friend.

*   *   *

Understanding others may feel a blessing, but understanding
thyself brings contentment.

*   *   *

Let the sun rise again; let the moon whisper your fate.
Let the sea wash its waves among your gate.
Time is too short, the wind so strong;
Allow your truth to guide you to where you belong.

*   *   *

So many situations arise that cause us to sit and ponder for hours, replaying circumstances over and over in our minds, trying to understand why this has occurred. The sooner we learn the patience we need to be in the now, the sooner we will understand ourselves. We open our thoughts to a higher knowing—a knowing how to understand situations and accept them without judgement. We accept that, sometimes, life has its own way of knowing what we should be doing with our lives and how. Open your heart; you will hear!

By learning to understand yourself, you are reaching into the core of knowing, and this can allow you the healing time you need in order to come to terms with what is occurring inside your soul.

At this time, allowing others to have an input is wise; All you need to remember is that your heart is your truth. You are in control of what you understand and how much you wish to deserve in life.

* * *

My intuition keeps nudging me to add this part in. Something very mysterious happened as I was writing this chapter. All I could think about was writing. I was going through yet another drastic change in my life, and suddenly my laptop charger was nowhere to be seen. This was a lesson to trust my own abilities to make a better future. I am strong, I am grateful, and I am beautiful.

As the week went on, my charger was still missing. I was anxious for the week ahead, unsure as to why my charger had gone missing at that exact moment. Following the consistent guidance of circumstances, I now sat there and understood.

Life hurts us, it rearranges us, and it tears us down and lifts us up. There is a deeper knowing to everything that occurs in your life—a deeper knowledge about the lessons you are learning over and over again or the lessons that are new to your world.

This journey of understanding yourself is one of the trickiest voyages you'll ever come across. You can control yourself and learn to accept what you can't control; you must be patient. Walk toward your dreams; don't rush for the finish line. Finding the answers doesn't involve rushing. If we look closely enough, we will see the answers slowly unfolding before our eyes. To understand this is to feel that your life is blessed by your presence.

* * *

Yesterday was clever; I wanted to change the world.
Today I am clever, so I'm changing myself.

*   *   *

TASK 2: JOURNAL

For this chapter's task, I want you to write to yourself. Start a journal, as well as your dream board. I want you to write and draw anything and everything that comes to mind about the hardships that have occurred in your life so far. Then I want you to write down a single reason why you should have given up when you were enduring these hardships. Some of your answers will be quite confrontational. Some you will want to hide from yourself. You will never heal completely if you don't love yourself entirely.

*   *   *

UNDERSTAND

If you want to awaken happiness in your world, you must start by
living a life that makes you happy and then radiate
your happiness outward.
If you want to eliminate suffering in the world, you must start by
eliminating the negative parts of yourself and then
radiate positivity outward.
Truly, the greatest power you have in this world is the power
of your own self-transformation.
It all starts with the man or woman in the mirror.

CHAPTER 3

CONTROL

Control, freedom, and inner peace

I have come to a realisation at a young age that nothing outside of ourselves is within our control. We can allow or deny another's words or actions to create us or destroy us. We can allow another the ability to change us or make us. Whether or not we give others this power is our choice; it is under our control, and it is a decision we must make.

Many must go through a darkness of truths. Many give up before they have learnt the lessons a situation has to offer. And many believe they have found their potential and there is no more to learn. There is always more to learn, always more to realise, always more to know about this dimension we all call life.

The truth is no one will ever stop growing. The moment you feel content with everything around you is the moment you will stagnate. Life is evolution, and evolution is life.

Controlling our emotions is a lesson we all need to learn—one that I myself am still learning and one of the hardest things to accomplish. This is a task that everyone in the world needs to conquer.

Wow oh wow, what a topic. Where and how to start? *Control* can you control yourself from exploding when something interferes with the peace of life's occurrences or when you're feeling anxious over something out of your control?

Still don't know how to control yourself from expressing these emotions or how to rid them from your body?

*   *   *

Exercise: Emotional Control

Lie down after reading this chapter; truly let yourself relax.

(This may be a difficult task if you don't do this often, but the feeling of accomplishing this small task is quite rewarding.)

Lie completely still; allow yourself to think about one emotion—not several, just one. Think about that emotion and what kind of feeling it creates in your body. As you are lying still, you are able to control this feeling. You have a choice; you can allow the feeling to control you and take over your being, or you can choose to shake that feeling.

I am teaching you a few affirmations of self-care and controlled response.

A raw emotion—a feeling that is quite strong—can override your being. If you are dishonest with yourself, then how do you expect the outside world to be truthful with you? Every action has its energized reaction.

Listen to yourself carefully, and trust that you are making the right choices for you.

Learning to control these feelings and parlaying this control into knowledge of how you wish to participate in the world is an enormous gift of life.

If we could control everything in our life, what would make us appreciate the good things?

Of course we are here to understand what we can and can't control, whilst staying knowingly faithful to our true, pure essence—our soul's purpose.

Imagine the feeling of control as if it were a river, an ever-changing flow of eternity from the universe. Even if we live in a world of peace, many tests will come our way to see if we have really learnt control—control on many levels.

Not much in life exists that we can truly control. But we must remember our strength and ability to walk tall through all that life throws at us. We must keep faith through the dark days. Like a storm through the night, everything has its cycles. Every cleansing must start again. Every action came from a reaction.

After you have learnt to control one of the feelings and you can lie still and calm, learn to accept and deny it in your body; this control is amazing.

Controlling this moment may take a few attempts; it may be slow and require patience. Accept each moment you lie there as living in the now, and see what it has to say; your soul never lies—no matter how much you don't want to hear what it has to say. It is speaking to you because it knows; when you have followed its guidance and moved forward a few steps, you will look back at this very moment, realising it was only the start of the most wonderful journey! This step will have you looking back years from now, believing in the true beauty of *you*.

*　*　*

Learning how to control one emotion, you start to explore through your soul like it's a trivia game. *You* understand that you have the answers within your own heart; you realise that it does talk to you.

You can ask it whatever you choose; you can start to *feel* which way you want to head in life.

To many, this part of your journey is an awakening in yourself, as if a light bulb has just turned on. You may feel as if you should have known this your entire life.

This part of healing can help you with the hardest decisions and even the easiest ones. It just has to be accurate and truthful.

Honesty is the strongest key to understanding self-enlightenment.

*　*　*

In my lessons through life, it took me months, even years, to come to the understanding of who I was and what I wanted to achieve in my life and to be entirely content with this understanding. As we stand today, I still have no idea, I am just purely blessed that I have allowed myself the journey of self-discovery and spiritual guidance. When I speak of spiritual guidance, I speak of my inner truth and understanding—our soul, our twin flame, our inner voice.

I sometimes found myself fighting against soul and ego. Ego is huge; ego can either make or break a soul.

So many people live in the ego lifestyle, forgetting their own true worth and living through judgement and fear. When I fight through my own ego, I feel the pain, the ache, the gut feeling so strongly that I can't bear to stand straight, that's when I learn control. I change my thoughts and, thus, my actions, creations, and reactions. I allow my mind, body and soul to discover the truth in acceptance and love. It's that easy; understanding yourself and controlling your actions.

*   *   *

Controlling our thoughts and actions gives us a feeling of empowerment on many levels. It teaches us inner peace and freedom; we learn how and how not to let a power trip override us.

You are in control of what you want and who you are. You are in control of deciding which people you choose to have in your life. You are in control of the way you feel.

So many factors exist that we cannot control. We can't control the way other people feel. If they choose to hurt us or ignore us or decide that they want to live life without us, we, within ourselves, need to learn to control the way their decisions make us feel.

Each of us has our own journey.

Sometimes we need to know in our hearts when it's time to let go of the old and worn-out so that the new can prosper.

You are never handed anything in life that you cannot fight through; sometimes the road you're on may just be a more difficult road than you once suspected.

Hold on for the ride; embrace all the feelings that fill your soul.

Believe in yourself and set yourself free.

*   *   *

Control allows change; change allows free will; free will allows peace; peace allows love and light; love and light allow happiness; happiness allows contentment; contentment allows fulfilment; fulfilment allows eternity.

Allowing your inner spirit to feel inner peace and freedom draws in nature's way to unfold its true beauty that it has waiting for you.

*   *   *

17

Task 3: Colouring Control

For this task, I want to see colour on paper of what you imagine control to be.

Put your drawing on your wall of faith and wisdom and allow the colours/creations to flow into your life.

As you imagine each night before you enter your dreams, think back to times you were struggling with some situation. Now allow the free will of your mind to accept this journey, as you can see you have come so far.

Colours are uplifting. I find that, when I'm having an off day, I will put on something bright—something a little chirpy to lift my spirits for the day. The power of positive thinking and empowering your own mind is the most needed and inexpensive gift to humankind.

*   *   *

Control

Nothing is yesterday imagining if tomorrow never came;
Treat this like control, and you'll never feel uneasy again.
Allow all outer circumstances to flow
Like the waves among the seas.
Control yourself, dear child;
Allow yourself to be free.
You cannot change what will happen,
But you can learn how to react.
You cannot change anybody else,
Only your own heart and soul; learn to relax.
Take a deep breath; let out all the sighs.
It's okay to express your feelings.
Just let it be, dear child.
No more outer lessons can occur deep within you.
Trust me on this subject; I only speak of truth.

CHAPTER 4

LISTEN

elcome to the life of opening your ears and allowing all knowledge to stick to your mind. Listening is a beautiful skill of any soul. Many of us are in too much of a rush to truly listen to what someone is saying. Or maybe we are at a different understanding, and therefore, we are not listening to what the truth is unravelling.

Be still. Stop. Listen. Accept. Love.

Using strong, positive words means having strong, positive vibrations.

Listening involves two worlds, the inner and the outer. "What is most important?" you ask.

I say that they're both important, a friends eye is a truthful mirror; although listening to yourself gets you to the core of your destiny, listening to another gives you the strength to reach the core.

This is where we combine the two as one and connect them, listening to yourself whilst respecting the other.

At this point, you will begin to understand what is holding you back in your life—what it is that isn't fitting anymore.

What feels right and what feels wrong?

It's okay to feel every emotion you feel. Don't be so hard on yourself, dear child. Life is for learning, and you're already halfway there.

19

*   *   *

Letting go doesn't mean that you're weak; it means you're strong enough to know that what you're letting go of doesn't fit in your world anymore.

*   *   *

Listening takes times, patience, understanding, pain, and happiness. It is heartfelt and *real.*

It doesn't involve just the ears but also the heart—the feelings that can change a world or destroy a world.

Out of love to yourself and the other, you must respect yourself enough to hear what is being said. Not everything you hear will fit in with what you feel is "right." Not every bad sentence will follow through to a bad outcome. We must learn, listen, and grow if we wish to better ourselves continually.

By listening to yourself, you are allowing yourself to open to growth, change, and self-discovery.

Every soul has his or her own destination, and I cannot speak of this enough; within it all and among the highest of understanding, we must always better ourselves from the person we were yesterday. We must carry open ears and a light heart; for this journey is where it will take you.

*   *   *

Listen to the beat of your own heart.

*   *   *

You will encounter many different worldly views/inspirations among your travels, many of which will fit so right in your "*own*" soul and many of which you will no longer be able to bear listening to. This is where you use your ability to choose your life, to accept what you wish to accept, and to listen closely enough to what others have to teach you.

Sometimes, all people really need is someone to listen to their theories, their hurts, and their happiness, without judgement or fear.

Every soul is entitled to freedom of speech, and we as humans owe it to our peers to listen with open hearts and open minds.

You now have a choice; you can walk away nodding your head, allowing what just happened to embrace you and enlighten you, or you can choose to walk away in haste with a "why me" attitude.

The choice is yours.

Listen.

* * *

In my views and beliefs, I love listening. Everyone has a story; everyone you encounter is put in your life for a reason. You may or may not know what that reason for a situation is. But as you listen to yourself, you'll understand when to control a situation or let the universe control you. Every encounter can change your life in some way if you let it.

I just can't help myself; as I'm writing, I get little nudges urging me to express to you my feelings. I have many thoughts and emotions, running both high and low. But the only one I am listening to is the one sitting with great strength just under my heart, telling me that I need to continue with this book. *Maybe finish a chapter or two, maybe many*, it's saying.

I trust myself to believe in the destiny of my dreams. When I look into the future, it sits brightly ahead of me. I know I will again have low times, but the knowledge I have encountered through self-discovery has given me the tools I need to prepare for life. Nothing and no one will ever stand in the way of my true happiness. I believe in myself; therefore, you believe in me—positive flow, positive outcome.

* * *

When you experience a gut instinct/sickening feeling in your stomach, listen to the first thought that comes to you as soon as you recognise the feeling. What is that thought?

Many times, we ignore the aching feeling in our gut, shrugging it off as something we ate. Or maybe we're just too much in a rush to notice our gut feelings at all. Regardless, you must listen; listen to yourself. You are in charge of the future, and only *you* have the power to make yourself happy.

So now flow through to understanding. Why you are feeling this way? Listen to what your gut is telling you. Write it down on paper. I find this to be the clearest way to seek out our emotions.

Listening takes patience, time, and endurance. In this universe, there is no race, no limit on time; things will happen as they are supposed to.

Through listening, you will only encounter happiness along your way, whilst ignorance ruptures the flow of the universe. By reacting from your ego of ignorance, you are already creating exactly what you don't want.

*   *   *

Your thoughts are your creations.

*   *   *

Listening is also believing, seeing, and opening your heart to the fulfilment that lies ahead. We all have many senses with which we can listen to ourselves.

- Listen through your *eyes*: When you look into someone's eyes you can see what he or she is saying; eyes are a truthful mirror.
- Listen through *instinctual feeling*: When you choose to listen by feeling your emotions, you desire the instinct inside you. Your instinct is usually the most common feelings that bring you on this journey.
- Listen through *touch*: Listen to others' reactions; feel their bodies, listening to their energy. Touch is a true sensation. It's a companionship like no other; the moment of touch gives of the feeling of love. Imagine this touch to be your own (yes, it's okay to love yourself).
- Listen through your *ears*: You're probably wondering, Is she going to mention the most obvious component of listening? Yes, I am, but I wanted to leave the ears until nearer the end of

the list because, in my opinion, your ears aren't your strongest listening tool. Yes, they are built to "hear," but this is not the same as listening.

- Listen through your *mouth*: Yes, you read correctly—mouth. Words, speech, communication—where would this world be without them? Oh, that's right; this world is starting to lose its mojo of truth. Communication is so important in any lifestyle, we must allow open communication in order to free ourselves. We must accept open truth, as if honesty was a blessing.

* * *

Listening is important. Learning is essential. Loving is admirable.

* * *

* * *

Task 4: Dream Page

In this task, I want you to create a dream page—a page that contains what you wish to achieve in a given period of time.

Allow your mind the freedom to create any image your heart desires. In this world, we create who we are. Creating who we are is allowing ourselves to understand what we want. By understanding what we want, we are able to control our thoughts so we can process positive energy. Controlling our thoughts with positive rhythm helps us to realise our true potential and listen to the beat of our own heart.

* * *

Listen

Intuition for our emotions, ears for opening,
Truth be heard when we see such an insightful thing
We have the tools necessary to live our lives with love.
We have so many messages coming through to us.
We are the generation that's prepared to stand for our way,
Prepared to fight for love, make a new way for the brighter day,
Speak softer with our voice and whisper through our speech,
Listen with our ears; are you listening close to me?
Angels are around, spirituality at its best.
Come to change what I know; now I must follow my quest.
Help the poor with the wisdom they already own,
Help the rich see their difference to what they know,
Help the children fight for their rights,
And help the earth bring back its delight.
We are the generation bound to make a change.
Listen with your heart, speak with kind words,
and know yourself today.

CHAPTER 5

CLEANSE

As you have discovered so many pleasures at this moment, you will now know cleansing to be a part of your journey.

You cannot move forward without experiencing good old cleanses through your entire body—your *mind*, *body*, and *soul*.

Know in your own heart when it is right to start your cleanse. You must first know it's for yourself, not the egos or opinions of others, also trying to understand what to cleanse.

These times will be hard; sometimes not all cleanses are enticing. I find that every cleanse has some sort of pain; we must accept the pain to appreciate the gain.

If you haven't poured your heart out in years, your cleansing period may even take years; in saying that, your strength will determine your fate.

I believe cleansing is completely natural; it is okay to rid the toxins from your body and to clear away the toxins that surround you.

Consider the lifestyle you live. Is it benefiting you? If so, how?

The most common areas of cleansing are friendships, relationships, negative beliefs, fear, and the past.

As we slowly rid ourselves of what no longer fits in our worlds, we slowly become content to allow the new in, at its own pace.

You may find it hard to say goodbye to some relationships, and others you may find a true blessing. Whatever the case, they all hold a place in your book of life.

Each and every failure is a lesson about what is new. We are always allowed to be better than we were before.

Accept more, and then you shall receive.

*   *   *

I find cleansing incredibly overwhelming; at times, it has made me feel off my track, like I wasn't supposed to be there. Other times, I have been fearless, with only a pure heart controlling my soul.

*   *   *

If you feel this way, you are not alone; you are supposed to go through all types of emotions as you discover your heart. It has many messages about yourself that you will start to understand. You will see yourself in a new light; you will appreciate all that you didn't before. The more you cleanse, the more you open all your chakras and live through your soul. Ego is now starting to fade.

Slowly, emotion may try and override you. Do not give in. Time does heal wounds; we must trust in this.

It takes *time* (as everything in this world does) and *courage* to cleanse your life. It's the rainy weather that will get you to the sunny days; it is all worth it.

Every tear is worth it. Every sad day seems so far in the past that you begin to rise again. You have felt sadness, so you're ready to enjoy happiness; you have endured hardship, so you finally start to allow belief into your life.

Be ready. Get ready. *Go.*

The simplest way to rid yourself of the toxins that are entering or already stable in your life is to know exactly what it is that you're cleansing. Communication is the way to be patient with you. Write your feelings down. Ask yourself some questions. What do you need to cleanse? Friends, toxins, negative thoughts, emotions? Are you working on making lifestyle changes? Do you need to open and detoxify your mind, body, and soul?

Sit back and look; re-evaluate what each of these brings to your life.

If any brings a feeling or emotion that you're trying to rid from your life, then allow that this is your one chance to make life how you wish it to be.

Your opportunity is now.

You should have underlying trust in your true friendships, your true companions with whom you share your life. So many people go through an entire life without realising the difference between a true companion and a companion who just is and the potential of the former.

When we surround ourselves with people who bring out our true potential, we allow ourselves to open our souls to their destinies.

It's a sad reality that some may never find their true friends, true relations, or true companions, as they're so wrapped up in the false lifestyle they're leading, in misleading emotions, or in finding a quick fix to help with loneliness.

Some are lucky enough to know their true friends their entire lives.

So now you have this knowledge; which would you prefer? Your choice always comes down to understanding yourself. Everything is related, and often decisions about the people we want or don't want in our lives brings us back to understanding what it is that we actually want. Now answer this question—what do you want and what is in your life that is stopping you from achieving what you want?

Pay close attention to the first thought that comes to mind; this is usually right.

Whatever the thought, learn a way to cleanse it from your life.

Yes, it'll be hard—another sad story to write in your book.

But—and this is a huge *but*—all of the right souls will enter your life once you allow the wrong ones to leave.

A positive exists for every negative.

After you've gained knowledge on the slow and empowering process of cleansing, your intuition will start speaking volumes. It'll start to answer your questions without your having to ask a single thing.

Our feelings are all connected; the more you cleanse, the more you can listen to the real you.

* * *

Ridding yourself of toxins and of pain allows you to understand why you were attracted to that pain in the first place. Many people believe digging into the past brings out too many sad memories—too many painful experiences that we all try so hard to ignore.

Eventually, we ignore ourselves; we expect to be fulfilled in the physical world, and we find ourselves incredibly let down when our expectations aren't fulfilled.

The power to deal with negative emotions is found in the strength imbedded in our hearts.

How can we ever understand ourselves if we're only ever happy, joyous, and gliding through life? We have to witness jealousy, heartache, vulnerability, hatred, and sadness to want peace and stillness is our lives. These feelings are strong; these feelings can and will override your entire life if you allow them the control. This is where I beg to differ.

Many, in this day and age, say things like, "Just move on." "It's the past. Let it go." My question to you is this—how do we just move on if we've never dealt with, cleansed ourselves, and forgiven the heartaches and pains from the past?

That to me is a mystery.

How do people live their entire lives ignoring the aching feeling in their hearts? Many answers belong to that question.

Many don't know themselves as happy people. Some won't ever trust themselves enough to continue where they are meant to be; they shadow themselves, believing whatever is broken inside of them will fix itself one day at a time with patience.

Wrong!

Cleansing is a beautiful, natural, efficient process in the growth of every soul. Allowing yourself to cleanse what doesn't fit—cleansing not only your physical emotions but your mind, body, and soul—allows freedom in your heart.

You start to feel unstuck, like you can see past the clouds that have lain so close above you.

When you're on the journey of cleansing, you will want to look at the sky and laugh. You will trust in yourself. You will believe you have made all the right decisions. Although the pain is strong, believe in the cycle of renewal.

Bless your soul. You are a true beauty, and you really have come so far. Well done!

I'll bet you're starting to feel better already. Good; then I am doing my job.

Write yourself a to-do list or write furiously about anything that comes to mind.

I am also feeling better. The feeling in my stomach is slowly starting to fade the more and more I write. Doing so is definitely my calling.

*   *   *

Of all the cleansing moments I have experienced throughout my life, three stand out most strongly in my memory.

The first cleanse was like a bursting out of my own bubble, I made a dramatic change, followed my soul, and moved to the sunshine coast, Queensland, at only fifteen. I followed the feeling in my own heart that led me to where I wanted to be. As many challenges followed, so did my independence. My light started to shine, and I was becoming a young woman.

The second cleanse was when I left my son's father. (Out of respect for the privacy of the situation between me and him, I will not be sharing much on this topic, I believe there are two sides to every story, and it is unfair for me to take part in telling his side. So all I'll say about this change is that, all the way through, I was cleansing and feeling I am talking for *my* experience and my journey. I hope you all understand.) This cleanse was the most intense; painful, yet enjoyable, journey of my life. It taught me some valuable lessons on trusting myself, allowing the old pain in my heart to heal, and understanding the process of letting it go. I also learnt about allowing the new to venture in and teach me all the lessons I had to learn; through human existence, about my own pains. And thus, I could evaluate who I was and what I wanted in life. This journey went on for a very long time. Troubled days and saddened nights; Let's just say I was a beautiful, confident girl who was growing up trying to be me in a world trying to be everybody else. As I fell In love, I lost who I was. In the end, I was a stranger to the world; a stranger to most of the people I knew; and, most painfully, a stranger to myself. I could not eat. I could not sleep. I was a walking mess in a screaming soul's body. The only way out was for me to write this book. This book stopped me from the endless doctors' appointments and the endless pain and suffering; it was the end to all my fears. For this hardship I grew to love myself endlessly and know exactly who I was, he is on his own journey as I am on mine, and I respect him for that.

I was now set *free*.

The third cleanse I want to share with you was an entire lifestyle change. I had to explore the deepest, ugliest parts of my core to enable the light to finally shine. I was a broken girl, with a dream so big and nowhere to run. I took a step forward. I believed in myself and continued to grow as an individual. Not every choice I made had a great outcome, but every choice I made gave me a lesson in the book of life. In the end the decision's I made have enabled me to understand life, feel unconditional love, compassion and true spiritual magic.

Nothing is ever beyond us, and nothing is ever behind us. We are here in the now, living for this exact moment and believing in the freedom of our peace.

* * *

Goodbye, my friend. I cry as you go; sometimes, we make mistakes.
For this, I may never know.
Some say I'm weak; in my heart, I'm strong. I'm strong enough to
know that, in my life, you don't belong.
So as the tears fall, before you enter your dreams, remember me,
my friend—a lesson from each other to believe.

* * *

How are you feeling now? Has this book rung a few bells in your ears?

I hope so. You know, it surprises me every day that I have the ability to write effortlessly. I used to think nothing of it; now, my dear readers, it's my life.

life may not always be what you wanted, you may never have had a chance to smile,
tomorrow is a new chapter, and i promise itll be worthwhile.
if we can smile for ourselves, we will smile alot;
give what you want, and youll recieve what you got. xo

Here is my book.

I needed a book after such a dramatic shift throughout my entire world. What I was experiencing was not just a common heartbreak; it felt as if my soul was birthing itself in human form. I couldn't understand.

I couldn't seem to find a book that offered me tools to help me with such changes that were easy enough. I was going through a transformation. I did not yet know the society we lived in. It was a physical, emotional, and, most importantly, spiritual cleanse.

I went through a startling shift on my own; I was learning one day at a time, one moment at a time.

I believe that, with family, friendships, and loving, supporting, and unconditional acceptance, anybody can succeed. No one is ever alone, if one has his or her mind as a best friend; this is what cleansing has taught me.

When you allow yourself the truth of what you wish to be, you start to see the beauty in the world, people are attracted to your aura, and you have many goals that you feel happy following.

You are living for your purpose—creating your existence.

*   *   *

This engaging feeling stopped me in my tracks, wanting more. I was trying too hard to understand what was happening to me.

Now its twenty-one months later, a drizzly night; I am eating my home-made lasagne and writing to you. What an *incredible* journey. One day, you will hear it all. As for now, I am writing a book that I feel I need to read.

I am still on my journey, as you are on yours. I don't know if we'll ever understand ourselves and our full potential.

As long as you're on the journey of self-discovery, you already know yourself a little more.

A part of my own cleanse was to write this book until the nagging feeling in my soul left. This chapter was quite uplifting for me; it showed me a tiny insight into my true heart's desire. Thank you for allowing me to express my deepest emotions, fears, and knowledge about life.

TASK 5: DRAWING EMOTIONS

In this task, I wish you to draw the emotions that are still lying deep within your heart; draw the colours and every feeling in depth.

On another piece of paper, draw your enlightened thoughts during the cleansing—show how you are feeling and what has changed. All emotions are to be in colour, as colour expresses your true identity.

Let yourself express freely; allow the rhythm of the universe to flow through you like the waves on the ocean shoreline.

Place your drawing on your dream board, and I will keep speaking to you soon. XO

*   *   *

The following is an affirmation I'd like you to put above your bed:

I allow all that needs to be cleansed from my mind, body, and spirit. I accept help from the universe and let go of what needs to be let go with the wind in the distance. Truth be told, my heart is free.

*   *   *

CLEANSE

When we follow a truth, a cleanse must follow;
If we wish for a better tomorrow,
We must forgive our lessons and remove our fears,
For these parts of our journeys are the most important of years.
Forget who we were yesterday, a mistake that had to be made,
A growth within ourselves; we choose our destiny today.
The now is all we need, the mind ever so still;
Sit peacefully and be our own best friend.
The journey feels so uphill.
One day, the sun will start to shine—
Shine through the clouds that once knew to hide—
A cleanse through your soul, your heart, and your mind;
Love yourself, trust yourself, live in your time.
The soul has no errors; once we rid all our fears,
The mind, body, and temple can live throughout the years.
It can shine the truth for all to see.
You say I'm wrong; I am prophecy.

CHAPTER 6

FORGIVENESS

*S*o far, we have recognised, understood, controlled, listened, and cleansed. We are now ready to face forgiveness; everything in this world deserves it.

Most of the time, we underestimate the power of forgiveness. To me, it is not a weakness; it's strength. It is the most enlightening feeling I have ever felt.

Forgiveness isn't just about forgiving the person for the heartache he or she has caused; it is forgiving and moving on.

I believe what is most important is to forgive yourself. We all make mistakes. We all feel ashamed at times. We all feel saddened by events, relieved, and vulnerable.

The only answer is to forgive, accept, and move forward with our lives. We must never stagnate, and we must rid ourselves of guilt, as we all did the best we could with what we had in the time we were given.

Forgiving is a true sentiment that allows your true inner growth to prosper.

How can you honestly ever love if you have never forgiven yourself for the last lost love? How can you ever have a best friend if you have never been your own best friend? How can you ever be truly happy if you have never forgiven yourself for being sad?

Forgiving is beautiful; it allows us to move on—to accept right from wrong and to grow and prosper.

If we choose not to forgive, we are choosing our own path of destruction—a path that will cause more pain, suffering, and grief. Forgiving does not make the mistake fade; it just enables the wrongdoer to correct his or her choice and become aware of the decisions that led to the unfolding of the given circumstances.

I believe we all have hurts in life that seem unforgivable. I also believe that everything we think is unforgivable is forgivable. We, in this society, have been raised to understand forgiving as a crossroads—as black and white. People often get lost in this thought, thinking, *No way; I cannot forgive such-and-such for what he or she has done or said.* Regardless of the choice anyone else has made, what is resenting the situation going to do? What is worrying over it going to achieve? Nothing but pain in your own heart; remember forgiving is the key that will open many doors.

*　　*　　*

Forgiving is allowing your own heart to let go. Whether or not what you are forgiving hurt you, you are now overcoming the power it has to control you.

You are forgiving the situation, forgiving the fear that allowed it there in the first place, forgiving yourself for doing things you have never done before, or even forgiving yourself for trusting yourself too much.

Whatever the case, we must remember that so much power comes with forgiveness.

This power is astonishing, enlightening, and uplifting. You are now forgiving someone or something for the damage that occurred to you. You are becoming a higher person by accepting the forgiveness and emotions it causes. You are releasing all toxins and living with the true beauty of deeper understanding.

As far as forgiveness goes, I'm still teaching myself. I'm still wondering how it occurs.

The biggest wake-up call for me; was noticing the changes that had been occurring within and around me for such a long period of time. I couldn't understand why people would forgive others so quickly or move on from situations without a second thought. As time went on, different happenings occurred. I witnessed purity. To forgive is to allow yourself the freedom to let go. Forgiving doesn't mean forgetting; forgiving means you are no longer allowing this worry to torment your peaceful mind.

Think of a painful memory as a leaf floating down the stream. You can watch it fade at the pace of the universe, accept what has happened, and peacefully walk away from it.

You, within yourself, will know where you are and who you are, as you're not a victim anymore.

What is still sitting inside yourself that you haven't forgiven?

Into your soul we go.

We automatically believe that only the "big" occurrences in our lives make an impact. Wrong—even the smallest of negativity can leave the biggest imprint in our subconscious. This cruel world is what makes us feel inadequate and different.

Forgive yourself first; how dare you tell yourself you're not worth it? How dare you tell yourself that you aren't good enough? Trust me; if you treat yourself this way, you will be your own worst enemy for eternity.

*   *   *

Sometimes, I think I am just repeating myself throughout this entire book. Am I going over and over what was already said? I don't believe so, as the more I write, the more knowledge I am opening up to, which I can put on paper as a beautiful book that will change so many lives. As you and I both know, we'll forever be teaching eachother about ourselves, others, and this dimension we all call life. Having this book on your shelf will give you a small smile, as you may know that, when times are tough or you're losing sight of any good that's occurring, you are not alone. We are all together; it is within my power to enable us to believe in ourselves.

* * *

You are beautiful; just because you have made a bad mistake does not mean you are a bad person. You must first acknowledge it, accept it, and apologize for it; then transform from it, forgive it, move on from it, and learn from it.

Life is beautiful, and we will forever face tragic moments, not because we deserve them or fear them but because we have a higher plan of self-awareness that allows us to fight through and reach the higher self. Some days will seem darker than the nights, but in the morning, when the sun awakens our minds, bodies, and souls, we will be fresh, renewed, and awakened.

Everything happens to us for a reason—a purpose you will all slowly understand.

* * *

TASK 6: FORGIVENESS PAPERS

In this task, I want you to write on paper occurrences that have appeared in your life that you need to forgive. I want to see words, lots of words. Remember freedom of speech, the importance of being honest with yourself, and love for another.

Next to the words or sentences, I want you to write how they made you feel and why. Following that, complete your sentences on how you wish to free these occurrences from your worry and forgive, so as to become stronger.

Grab a new piece of paper. I want you to write down all the emotions you are feeling towards the new you. I want colour and some of your favourite affirmations and truths in the most vibrant colours you can find.

Complete both these sheets of paper.

With the fears-and-emotions piece of paper, I want you to go into nature—somewhere you feel content and comfortable. *Burn* this piece and allow the smoke to fly with the wind whilst your thoughts are exhaled from your mind and heart. Now go home. Have a cleansing sea salt bath or shower and—voila—a cleanse can be completed.

As for the second piece of paper, insert it on your dream wall. This is where you're headed in life; this is where you will force your mind to see the inspirational future—the prosperity your heart and soul will bring.

Looking at this dream wall, you are slowly constructing and witnessing so many changes, you will start to see the light at the end of the tunnel. This is called creative visualisation; what we see, we believe.

FORGIVENESS

So many say to forgive is to accept what's been done.
You have it all wrong, dear children. Forgiveness is the one,
The one key to eternity, to happiness, and to peace—
The one lesson we all must learn to set our souls free.
Forgiving is allowing yourself to feel no more pain;
Letting go of circumstances, there is much to be gained.
So as you go to sleep tonight, think of all you wish to change,
The change within yourself, and watch the ego fade.
I forgive you, as you forgive me;
Let's allow peace on earth and the freedom to let it be.

CHAPTER 7

HEAL

I wonder, do we truly ever know when we are healed? Do we ever experience beautiful contentment?

I believe the answer is yes. We are healed when we realise our truest potential, when we understand what our soul is saying to us, when we make choices for ourselves and not for the ego or judgement of another.

Healing can take months and years to complete. Many may never know how to heal themselves, but the true beauty about humanity is that we all have a choice; we can choose the way we wish to live our lives.

A long time ago, I would sit in my room and cry; I would cry for many reasons but not one reason that was worth that many tears. I wish that, back then, I would have had a book like this to give me the simple tools to heal myself, to understand myself, and to get to know myself a little better.

I wanted to be own my best friend, and I believe that, once you can be your own best friend, you will have healed.

We were born to be ourselves. So many people have it wrong; they wish to be others, whilst wasting away their own beauty and light.

* * *

43

Healing is a process that will never stop, as life won't ever be just easy. When we choose to go toward the things in life that we want or cherish deeply, along with this movement comes new lessons, new journeys, which won't always be what we wanted. We so often paint a perfect picture of what we wish something to be.

We forget that people are living and situations do occur.

I believe that, when you are healed of your recent and past pains, handling circumstances that would have previously brought you down will be easier. You learn to fight a little harder, become a little more patient, and grow to understand that we can't control everything. With this knowledge, we accept life for what it is—a blessing.

We understand where we want to be in life, we begin to unravel the many creative layers of our own beings, and we *finally* start to live with soul, unafraid of what might become and eager to know more.

We have many questions, many of which this book will awaken. But I know it has many truths that can no longer be ignored. We are entering into a dimension on earth that will rebirth our souls and awaken our hearts.

Healing is allowing your heart to feel pure and free; it allows your potential to soar and your humanly existence to be unforgettable. Strive to better yourself from who you were yesterday and teach yourself for tomorrow.

Healing yourself leaves you feeling content with your life. Don't feel overwhelmed if you are still waking up, still experiencing changes, or still trying to understand chapter 3.

You are not alone.

Give yourself the opportunity to be that person, for you will never know otherwise. Life is too short; once we leave this world, nothing can be undone. So enjoy the ride and hold on tight.

* * *

As I sit writing this beloved book, I am going through changes. The year is 2013, and in my knowledge and beliefs, this year is powerful; this is the year to allow yourself to prosper and become the person you wish to be, finally gaining the strength to let your own star shine.

I walked alone, not because I had to but because I chose to. The ones who change the world do not follow; they make a path where the grass is too long. The road is never too short, and the journeys are yet to be heard of. Be different. Be daring. Be real.

As I continue, I'd like to discuss what happens when something occurs in your life that makes you feel angry. What about when you feel vulnerable to situations you don't want to be in? Do you choose to accept it or deny it?

Accepting is healing; denying is ignoring.

Understand the difference. If everything in life we choose to do we choose out of love and purest intentions, how can we ever want to ignore ourselves, the truest core of our being? We need to accept what is happening and understand it, speak with kind words, and heal through the painful process.

Healing leaves you feeling good; you experience a feeling of accomplishment, power, and love. You appreciate the smallest things— the trees, birds, water, and the simplicity of the air we breathe in.

Some situations leave us feeling sick to our stomach; we feel an ache in our gut, and we feel nausea; we feel off and out of balance. By understanding these emotions, you can start to research what you wish to do to enable yourself to release these feelings, thereby healing yourself with love and care.

Heal, heal, heal.

Never take on much more than you can handle. I am no doctor, psychologist or counsellor, but I did heal myself; I did go through hell and back, suffering all sorts of aches, pains, and inside traumas. The list really could go on.

Always listen to your body over the advice of another. Your soul and heart know exactly what you need to do.

* * *

- *So often, we underestimate the power of a kind word, a loving touch, and a warm welcome. In one day, it would make the world go round.*
- *Mistakes are for those who wish to be perfect. I say they are all in need of the lessons we ought to learn.*
- *You don't stop laughing as you grow old; you grow old when you stop laughing.*

* * *

So who are you?

Out of all this searching, have you come to love yourself? Better yet, have you come to understand yourself a little closer to the core?

You are important. You are more important than anyone else on this earth. If you are a mother, you are more important than your child; without yourself intact, how can you raise your child, providing the best of what he or she needs?

If you are a friend, you are more important than your friend; how can you give out what you don't have within you?

If you are a daughter or son, you are more important than your parent; as long as you make the choices that you yourself are proud of, you must follow your own heart.

If you are a partner or spouse or lover, you are more important than your other; if you don't love yourself, how can you love another?

Get my gist. You are the most important person in your life.

You must look after you before you look after another.

* * *

Task 7: Something Relaxing

In this task, I ask you to try something you haven't tried before—something you find relaxing, calming, and rejuvenating.

Food for thought—try meditation, yoga, art classes, exercise; the list really could go on. Just find something that brings out the best in you, leaving you feeling refreshed.

Take pictures of your newfound hobbies. Write a brief message about the experience and place it on your dream wall. You see, now it's becoming closer to realising *your* potential—not your partner's, not your parents', not your children's, and not your relations' or friends'—just *yours*.

*   *   *

If you have read this far into the book, thank you. You don't know what it means to me to help heal your soul; we are all here together as one, to live in a pure environment.

*   *   *

Heal

Let's change the way we sleep, change the way we speak,
Speak softer with our words and wiser through our speech.
We are the generation starving for hope;
Strenuous futures and hardships to follow.
With unity and peace this world could be
A truth, a love, a deep prophecy.
The gods above in the heaven's realms
Sit by, watching all the darkness fill;
It's not up to them but humanity down below
To enrich and love again, something we've never known.

CHAPTER 8

YOU AND YOURSELF

You.

*D*o you understand yet that you are the most important person you will ever meet? Do you know that, if you ignore yourself for too long, you will take longer to heal the soul?

So many of us forget that we are the most important; so many people put themselves last in order to help another.

I myself have been a victim of this type of self-abuse. I constantly ran around looking after every person who needed me; I relentlessly faced obstacles that were not my battles, just because I am the healer I am. For so long, I put myself under every person I had met. Why? Only I will ever know. You slowly start to find yourself in a world full of false identities. This is the time I started to awaken, to see everything for what it was. I was in control of myself. Therefore, what gave another the right to my time, my body, or my healing abilities without my consent?

If you answered nothing, that's right.

You see, as a human being, you are hungry; you feed yourself. If you are thirsty, you supply yourself a drink. The same flow happens surrounding the way life teaches and reaches at us.

If you are a parent, you are more important than your child; a happy parent means a happy baby. If you are a friend, you need to be your own friend first; if you don't like who you are as a person, how do you expect anyone else to? If you are a lover, you must love yourself first. And so it goes. Get my gist?

We need to make sure we are our number-one fan, our number-one love, and the number-one person we can rely on. We have to live with ourselves for the rest of our days—not a day away and not a day before.

*   *   *

We so often are rushing to help another or look after the needs of another or even help heal another. We are here to share, love, and prosper together. But who are we to allow ourselves to depend that much on others' needs before our *own*?

Because of the kind of person I am, I would happily help anyone; but now I have come to understand where my energy is wanted and appreciated.

Sometimes, before we think of the needs of others, we must think first about ourselves. If we are sacrificing our own hard work and hard-earned accomplishments to help the other, then this is where we stop. You must stop, stand, be still, and accept that it's okay to say no. It's okay to look within, towards our own needs before we announce to the world that we're available.

A truer soul is one who knows him or herself or is finding him or herself—someone who is living in truth and gaining independence. You must rely on yourself whilst allowing the support of others.

After reading this entire book, we may feel like it's not sinking in to our brains. Yet, as we rest our eyes later in the night, we slowly remember everything we need to.

I hope this book has given you a clear insight into healing yourself naturally. As I am still learning, I do know there are plenty of other ways to go about self-healing. As I said before, I could never find a book to satisfy my needs—a book that really talked about the truest of emotions without judgement or fears.

So as we sit now, we have gone through our heartache. We have experienced sunshine; we've fought off storms and witnessed the pure essence of a dragonfly. We are forever grateful for our existence.

At times, life will be hard, and I believe this book won't be the end for you; really, it's just the beginning.

I will promise you one thing; if you continue to follow your heart, it will all be worthwhile.

You need to face your fears head-on; face the happiness within yourself and create yourself from the inside out. Looks do fade; beauty within showers forever.

You are a beautiful person. You are on an untravelled road. Keep going.

Everything will be okay.

*   *   *

Task 8: Spoil Yourself

In this task, I wish you to spoil yourself; do something that makes you happy.

Don't think too hard about how you are going to do it; just do it. You deserve it.

Bless your beautiful soul and let the light shine through.

*   *   *

You and Yourself

When you know yourself, you know yourself completely;
You know everything about you from the top of your head to the
bottom of your feet.
You learn to nourish your own world,
Treat it with unconditional care;
You learn who you are and who is always there.
Every soul we encounter had a lesson along the way,
A lesson in which it learnt to grow or stagnate,
So the choice is yours; you can stay or go.
The lessons—have they taught you? You must live and grow.
Grow to know your worth, love all you are;
You, you're extremely powerful, as we all were here from the start,
As evolution went round, its six cycles on mist.
We can now love who we are with all the courage we need.
Love your heart, your soul, and your mind.
Then you will see that your outside will shine.

CHAPTER 9

TO THE FUTURE AND BEYOND

"*L*ife is a highway; I'm gonna ride it all night long." I bet this song has already come into your mind and you're ready to get up on the table and boogie.

This song is a song that I will always think of when I'm going through a change in my life. You see, at this present time, I find every experience (painful or joyous) uplifting. I have reached the understanding that everything happens for a reason. I choose how I wish to live my life, what I let control me, and what I wish to define me.

The new beginnings that are still unknown to us are sometimes the most rewarding. When we know nothing in our future, we have no expectations of any situation. We learn that nothing can make us happy, nor can anything take our happiness away. We learn to only create it for ourselves. We control who we are, and our future becomes closer and more real.

Gaining strength, respect, and love for yourself empowers you to make decisions that you feel right about; it enables you to smile when you feel like crying or laugh when you feel a big ache inside.

It is okay to talk about the way you feel—to express your sorrows, to rejoice in your happiness. You can be whatever it is you wish to be.

Believe in the beauty of your own dreams; the future will belong to you.

The future is yours. You hold the key; you write the story.

As we sit now, we have the past behind us, the future in front of us, and the now *right here.*

Let's let the past go, be free in the here and now, and know that the future will unfold when we make the choice to change ourselves.

I have supported your darkest nights and loneliest days; it is now up to you to continue on the path of self-understanding.

* * *

Have the courage to accept the past as the past,
The courage to live here in the now,
And the wisdom to dream for the future.

* * *

Task 9: Go and Do

The last task for this book is this:

You know all those things you've always wanted to do. Go and do them.

Peace. Love. Gratitude.

* * *

To the Future and Beyond

It's you and I who make the world a better place;
Humanity's dying, children are crying, the world sickens to death.
Learn to stand tall when everything falls and
rise to the dreams of your head.
It's never too late to start today, as tomorrow is never yours.
Yesterday is gone; today is all we have, so live freely, explore.
We won't know the chapter if we don't turn the page;
We won't accept who we are if we stay and stagnate.
It's never the answers we already knew
But the undiscovered roads that we don't have any clue.
They teach us strength when we have nothing else;
They teach us to love more freely, more so ourselves.
The choice is always ours.
Never let another speak the road that you discovered.
It's too short to wake with regrets. Never put yourself down.
Learn to love unconditionally and respect.
Look into the mirror natural as can be;
You will see the beauty in your eyes when you set your soul free.

About the Author

*S*tay-at-home young mother and earth wanderer Nikki Rowe was born in Sydney, New South Wales, in late 1990. She was raised in Brisbane, Queensland, until she followed her journey to the Sunshine Coast at fifteen. There she still resides, living with her beautiful three-year-old son; enjoying the simplest pleasures of the earth and digging deeper into the hidden truths of this earth.

She has a view to change the world through healing it and bringing alive a higher consciousness. With every word she speaks, she brings a new type of knowledge to her peers, to children, and to our next generation—finally opening our hearts to live with love.

Writing is a passion on which she thrives. She wishes to create peace and awareness that every soul has a journey, every feeling is never really ours, and every thought we have creates our future.

Life hasn't always been easy. She has fought battles, exceeded beliefs anyone could imagine, and focused always on the truth, unafraid to stand alone and willing to try anything to complete her story of life.

So the journey begins . . .

*   *   *

Email Nikki at:
Mail Nikki at:
Book Nikki to speak at your event through:
Nikki's website links.

Made in the USA
Columbia, SC
15 August 2020